WE READ ABOUT
FOSSILS

By Tracy Vonder Brink and Madison Parker

A Lighthouse Book

SEAHORSE PUBLISHING

Parent and Caregiver Guide

Reading aloud with your child has many benefits. It expands vocabulary, sparks discussion, and promotes an emotional bond. Research shows that children who have books read aloud to them have improved language skills, leading to greater school success.

I Read! You Read! books offer a fun and easy way to read with your child. Follow these guidelines.

Before Reading

- Look at the front and back covers. Discuss personal experiences that relate to the topic. Make predictions about the book.
- Scan the *Glossary* at the back of the book. Talk about any words that are new to your child
- If the book will be challenging or unfamiliar to your child, read it aloud by yourself the first time. Then, invite your child to participate in a second reading.

During Reading

 Have your child read the words beside this symbol. This text has been carefully matched to the reading and grade levels shown on the cover.

 You read the words beside this symbol.

- Stop often to discuss what you are reading and to make sure your child understands.
- If your child struggles with decoding a word, help them sound it out. If it is still a challenge, say the word for your child and have them repeat it after you.
- To find the meaning of a word, look for clues in the surrounding words and pictures.

After Reading

- Praise your child's efforts. Notice how they have grown as a reader.
- Use the *Comprehension Questions* at the back of the book.
- Discuss what your child learned and what they liked or didn't like about the book.

Most importantly, let your child know that reading is fun and worthwhile. Keep reading together as your child's skills and confidence grow.

TABLE OF CONTENTS

Chapter 1: Fossils 4

Chapter 2: Body Fossils 6

Chapter 3: Trace Fossils 9

Chapter 4: How Fossils Form 13

Chapter 5: Finding Fossils 19

Chapter 6: Fabulous Fossils 25

Glossary 30

Index 31

Comprehension Questions 31

FOSSILS

The word *fossil* comes from the Latin word for "dug up" or "unearthed." Fossils are **remains** or traces of ancient life that are at least 10,000 years old. They are **preserved** in rock, soil, or amber.

Keichousaurus *is a reptile that lived in China about 240 million years ago.*

FOSSIL FACT

The fossil record goes back more than three billion years. Looking at these fossils gives us a peek into Earth's past.

Fossils found around the world make up the fossil record. Paleontologists are scientists who use the fossil record to understand ancient life. They divide fossils into two main groups—body fossils and trace fossils.

BODY FOSSILS

A body fossil was once part of an animal or a plant. Hard parts such as bones, teeth, and wood often become fossils. In fact, bones and teeth are the most common fossils found. But eggs, skin, and leaves may also become fossils.

Body fossils help paleontologists figure out how an ancient animal or plant looked. A fossil of a plant can show how big it grew. The shape of a tooth helps us know if an animal ate plants or meat. Bones tell scientists if an animal walked on two or four legs.

Paleontologists rarely find a complete skeleton with all its parts attached. So, they must puzzle out how the bones might have fit together. A discovery of new fossils may change our idea of how a dinosaur or other ancient animal looked and behaved.

FOSSIL FACT

When *Iguanodon* fossils were first discovered, paleontologists thought this dinosaur had a spike on its nose. Later discoveries revealed that the spike belonged on its thumb.

8

TRACE FOSSILS

ADULT Trace fossils are what living things left behind while they were alive. Footprints, nests, and even poop are all trace fossils. They show the movement and activity of past life.

Footprints

Fossilized footprints give clues to how and where animals moved long ago. A group of the same kind of tracks might mean the animals traveled together in a herd. Tracks spaced farther apart suggest that an animal was running—possibly toward a meal or away from danger.

FOSSIL FACT

A tail mark is also a trace fossil. A tail mark along with footprints might mean the animal dragged its tail as it walked.

FOSSIL FACT

Dinosaurs built nests on the ground much the same way some of today's birds do. They used their feet and claws to scrape out and pile up soil.

Fossilized Troodon nests have also been found on Egg Mountain.

Nests

Trace fossils show that some dinosaurs built nests on the ground for their eggs. At a **site** known as Egg Mountain in the state of Montana, United States, paleontologists uncovered 14 bowl-shaped nests built by *Maiasaura* dinosaurs. The nests were over six feet (two meters) wide.

Poop

Coprolite is the scientific name for fossilized poop. Coprolite gives clues to what an ancient animal ate. Bones found in coprolite show the animal was a meat-eater. Seeds or bark suggest that it ate plants.

HOW FOSSILS FORM

Conditions must be exactly right for fossils to form. Most living things completely **decay** after they die, so very few become fossils. In fact, scientists think that less than one percent of all animals are fossilized. That's about one bone in a billion.

Body Fossils

When an animal dies, its soft parts rot away and leave its bones, teeth, and other hard parts. To fossilize, these hard parts must be quickly buried by **sediment** such as mud, sand, or volcanic ash.

FOSSIL FACT

Sometimes, animals become trapped in landslides. Scientists think that collapsing sand dunes in Central Asia's Gobi Desert buried a group of dinosaurs.

ADULT   It takes more than being buried to become a fossil. Water must collect around the bones, teeth, and other hard parts. Over millions of years, **minerals** in the water replace the hard parts and leave behind a copy. A fossil is rock—not bone or tooth—but it looks just like the original.

15

Mold Fossils

Sometimes, a buried bone completely **dissolves** before a fossil can form. But it leaves a bone-shaped space. If water fills the space and **deposits** minerals, the minerals can create a fossil shaped like the bone that used to be there. This kind of fossil is called a mold fossil.

Ammonites were shelled sea creatures that lived 150 million years ago.

FOSSIL FACT

Colorado's Picket Wire Canyonlands in the United States have the most dinosaur tracks in North America. More than 1,900 fossilized dinosaur footprints have been found there.

Fossilized Tracks

ADULT

Fossilized footprints may form where a living creature stepped in soft mud. The tracks harden and are buried in sediment. Like other fossils, the tracks then fill with water and minerals.

17

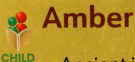

Amber

Ancient insects are sometimes found in amber. Long ago, **resin** oozed from a tree's bark. A bug flew, fell, or crawled into it and became stuck. More layers of resin covered it and hardened. The tree fell and was buried in layers of sediment. Then, the resin fossilized into amber—with the bug preserved inside.

FOSSIL FACT

Scientists doubt that DNA could really be pulled from a mosquito fossilized in amber, like it is in the movies. DNA breaks down too fast and wouldn't last hundreds of millions of years.

FINDING FOSSILS

FOSSIL FACT

In 2021, a boulder fell from a cliff and cracked open near a beach in northeastern England. Inside was a 326 million-year-old fossil of a giant millipede.

ADULT Fossils form deep below many layers of rock, but the forces that change Earth bring them to the surface. Some rock layers are uplifted into mountains. **Weathering** and **erosion** wear down rock and expose fossils. Landslides can also reveal buried fossils.

Fossils form in sedimentary rock, so paleontologists use **geologic** maps to locate those kinds of rocks. They focus on places where fossils are more likely to be exposed, such as hillsides, river valleys, and cliffs.

FOSSIL FACT

Paleontologists also look for fossils based on the age of rocks. A scientist studying fossils that formed 200 million years ago would look in an area with rocks that old.

20

ADULT
When paleontologists go to an area to find fossils, they walk around and look at the ground. If they do find a bit of fossil, they brush away the dirt around it to see if more may be buried.

Paleontologists use shovels, rock hammers, and other tools to remove each fossil they find. They wrap it in a plaster cast, like a doctor wraps a broken bone. The cast protects the fossil as it's dug out and moved to a lab or museum.

Finding Fossils Underground

ADULT

Because they work below Earth's surface, miners find fossils by accident. In 2011, a miner in Alberta, Canada, was digging a tunnel. He uncovered a dinosaur that had been buried for about 110 million years. The armored dinosaur, part of a group of dinosaurs called nodosaurs, was the best-preserved one of its kind ever found.

Fossils and You

You don't have to be a scientist to look for fossils. Check out a library book or visit a museum to learn how to spot them. On a fossil hunt, take what you would for any outdoor adventure—comfortable shoes, sunscreen, a hat, water, and a phone. Then head to places where fossils are more likely to be found, such as a creek bed or a beach, and use your eyes.

Not all places allow you to take home any fossils you may find. Check the rules for your area before you go.

FABULOUS FOSSILS

Sue's bones tell paleontologists that she lived to be about 28 years old.

Sue

Sue is the nickname of a *Tyrannosaurus rex* on display in the Field Museum in Chicago, Illinois, in the U.S. It's named after the woman who found it in 1990. Sue is the largest and most complete *T. rex* fossil found so far.

Archaeopteryx

Fossils show that *Archaeopteryx* had feathers like a bird but also had teeth, claws, and a bony, dinosaur-like tail. Was *Archaeopteryx* the first bird? Or was it more closely related to dinosaurs? Scientists aren't sure.

Unlike today's birds, Archaeopteryx had a full set of teeth.

Titanosaurs were huge, but they only ate plants.

Titanosaur

ADULT

    Titanosaurs were a group of huge dinosaurs that lived about 100 to 95 million years ago. The largest ever found stretches 122 feet (37 meters) long. That's longer than three school buses placed end to end!

Taung Child

In 1924, a fossilized skull about three million years old was found by miners in Taung, South Africa. The skull belonged to a young child. It was one of the first fossils of early humans to be found in Africa.

Marks on Taung Child's skull suggest the child was attacked by an eagle.

ADULT   More than 10,000 dinosaur fossils have been unearthed by scientists since 1824. Fossils have been found everywhere—even on Mount Everest, the highest mountain on Earth. Paleontologists think there are many more to be discovered. Will you find one?

GLOSSARY

decay (di-KAY): to be slowly broken down by natural processes

deposits (di-PAH-zitz): places or lays down; unloads something in a place

dissolves (di-ZAHLVZ): mixes one or more solids and liquids until the solid becomes part of the liquid; disappears into a liquid

erosion (i-ROH-zhuhn): the wearing down of a surface, such as rock, by wind, rain, ice, and other natural forces

geologic (jee-uh-LAH-jik): connected to the scientific study of Earth, including its rocks and soil

minerals (MIN-ur-uhlz): solids that form naturally in the Earth and that do not come from an animal or a plant

preserved (pri-ZURVD): kept something in good condition or in its original state

remains (ri-MAYNZ): the parts of something left behind; parts of ancient things that have survived

resin (REZ-in): a sticky substance made by some trees

sediment (SED-uh-muhnt): natural material, such as rocks or decayed plant matter, that is broken down and carried by wind, water, or other natural processes and that settles in layers

site (site): the place where something happened or is located

weathering (WETH-ur-ing): the process of being broken down by contact with natural forces such as wind, water, or ice

INDEX

amber 4, 18

Archaeopteryx 26

coprolite 12

Egg Mountain 11

mold fossils 16

nodosaurs 23

paleontologists 5, 7, 8, 11, 20-22, 25, 29

Sue 25

Taung Child 28

titanosaurs 27

COMPREHENSION QUESTIONS

1. Fossils found around the world make up _____.
    a. geologic maps
    b. the fossil record
    c. coprolite

2. What kinds of fossils were once parts of animals?
    a. body fossils
    b. trace fossils
    c. amber

3. What kinds of fossils show the movement or activity of past life?
    a. body fossils
    b. trace fossils
    c. amber

4. True or False: Scientists think that less than one percent of all animals are fossilized.

5. True or False: Scientists often find complete fossilized skeletons.

Answer Key: 1. b 2. a 3. b 4. True 5. False

Written by: Tracy Vonder Brink and Madison Parker
Design by: Under the Oaks Media
Series Development: James Earley
Editor: Kim Thompson

Photo credits: Alones: p. cover; Mark Brandon: p. 4; Gorodenkoff: p. 5; Nadezda Murmakova: p. 7; kamomeen: p. 8; Milan Sommer: p. 8; Stock for you: p. 9; Sergio Foto: p. 10; Maksim Shchur: p. 11; Ibe van Oort: p. 12; Potapov Alexander: p. 13;ESB Basic: p. 14; Nuntiya: p. 15; Carolina Jaramillo: p. 16; Nicholas Courtney: p. 17; Matteo Chinellato: p. 18; s_licciardello: p. 19;Popel Arseniy: p. 20; Evgeny Haritonov: p. 21;paleontologist natural: p. 22; Goldsithney: p. 24; EQRoy: p. 25; Natalia van D: p. 26; schusterbauer.com: p. 27; Puwadol Jaturawutthichai: p. 28; Goldsithney: p. 29;

Library of Congress PCN Data
We Read About Fossils / Tracy Vonder Brink and Madison Parker
I Read! You Read!
ISBN 979-8-8904-2492-1 (hard cover)
ISBN 979-8-8904-2496-9 (paperback)
ISBN 979-8-8904-2500-3 (EPUB)
ISBN 979-8-8904-2504-1 (eBook)
Library of Congress Control Number: 2023918561

Printed in the United States of America.

Seahorse Publishing Company

seahorsepub.com

Copyright © 2024 SEAHORSE PUBLISHING COMPANY

All rights reserved. No part of this publication may be reproduced, stored in a retrieval system or be transmitted in any form or by any means, electronic, mechanical, photocopying, recording, or otherwise, without the prior written permission of Seahorse Publishing Company.

Published in the United States
Seahorse Publishing
PO Box 771325
Coral Springs, FL 33077